SAVE SAVE SAVE
WATER WATER WATER W
DRINK DRINK D
NE WINE WINE W

SAVE SAVE SAVE
WATER WATER WATER
DRINK DRINK DRINK
WINE WINE WINE

SAVE SAVE SAVE
TER WATER WATER W
INK DRINK DRINK D
NE WINE WINE W

SAVE SAVE SAVE
WATER WATER WATER
DRINK DRINK DRINK
WINE WINE WINE

SAVE
WATER
DRINK
WINE

summersdale

Drink wine, and you will sleep well. Sleep, and you will not sin. Avoid sin, and you will be saved. Ergo, drink wine and be saved.

Medieval German proverb

SAVE WATER DRINK WINE

Copyright © Summersdale Publishers Ltd, 2012

Summersdale Publishers Ltd
46 West Street
Chichester
West Sussex
PO19 1RP
UK

www.summersdale.com

Printed and bound in the Czech Republic

ISBN: 978-1-84953-269-3

Substantial discounts on bulk quantities of Summersdale books are available to corporations, professional associations and other organisations. For details telephone Summersdale Publishers on (+44-1243-771107), fax (+44-1243-786300) or email (nicky@summersdale.com).

Good wine is a good familiar creature if it be well used.

William Shakespeare, *Othello*

Wine is a living
liquid containing no
preservatives.

Julia Child

Burgundy makes you think of silly things, Bordeaux makes you talk of them and champagne makes you do them.

Jean Anthelme Brillat-Savarin

Is your Englishman so
expert in his drinking?

William Shakespeare, *Othello*

Wine is bottled poetry.

Robert Louis Stevenson

I must get out of these
wet clothes and into a
dry Martini.

Robert Benchley

I spent ninety per cent of my money on wine, women and song and just wasted the other ten per cent.

Ronnie Hawkins

Consuming wine
in moderation daily
will help people to
die young as late as
possible.

Dr Philip Norrie

Wine, taken in moderation, makes life, for a moment, better, and when the moment passes life does not for that reason become worse.

Bernard Levin,
From the Camargue to the Alps

Quickly, bring me a beaker of wine, so that I may wet my mind and say something clever.

Aristophanes

I never drink water;
that is the stuff that
rusts pipes.

W. C. Fields

It is most absurdly said, in popular language, of any man, that he is disguised in liquor; for, on the contrary, most men are disguised by sobriety.

Thomas de Quincey, *Confessions of an English Opium-Eater*

When I read about
the evils of drinking, I
gave up reading.

Henny Youngman

The sharper is the
berry, the sweeter is
the wine.

Proverb

Sorrow can be alleviated by good sleep, a bath and a glass of wine.

St Thomas Aquinas

I have enjoyed great health
at a great age because
every day since I can
remember I have consumed
a bottle of wine except when
I have not felt well. Then I
have consumed two bottles.

A Bishop of Seville

Wine is the most healthful and most hygienic of beverages.

Louis Pasteur

For when the wine is in, the wit is out.

Thomas Becon, *Catechism*

Champagne is one of the
elegant extras in life.

Charles Dickens, *Household Words*

Too much Chablis can make you whablis.

Ogden Nash

A hard drinker, being at table, was offered grapes at dessert. 'Thank you,' said he, pushing the dish away from him, 'but I am not in the habit of taking my wine in pills.'

Jean Anthelme Brillat-Savarin,
The Physiology of Taste

Wine is the most
civilised thing in
the world.

Ernest Hemingway

The soft extractive note of an aged cork being withdrawn has the true sound of a man opening his heart.

William S. Benwell,
Journey to Wine in Victoria

He's such a connoisseur. He not only knows the year the wine was made but he can tell you who stamped on the grapes.

Edith Gwynn

A man ought to get drunk at least twice a year… so he won't let himself get snotty about it.

Raymond Chandler

I envy people who drink —
at least they know what to
blame everything on.

Oscar Levant

I have taken more out of alcohol than alcohol has taken out of me.

Winston Churchill

There comes a time in every woman's life when the only thing that helps is a glass of champagne.

Bette Davis

A drink a day keeps
the shrink away.

Edward Abbey

Teetotallers lack the sympathy and generosity of men that drink.

W. H. Davies

I know I'm drinking myself to a slow death, but then I'm in no hurry.

Robert Benchley

Then trust me there's
nothing as drinking
So pleasant on this side
of the grave:
It keeps the unhappy
from thinking,
And makes e'en the valiant
more brave.

**Charles Dibdin,
'Nothing Like Grog'**

Penicillin cures
but wine makes
people happy.

Sir Alexander Fleming

My grandmother is over eighty and still doesn't need glasses. Drinks right out of the bottle.

Henny Youngman

Claret is the liquor for boys; port, for men; but he who aspires to be a hero… must drink brandy.

Samuel Johnson

I feel sorry for people who don't drink. When they wake up in the morning, that's as good as they're going to feel all day.

Frank Sinatra

… good company, good wine, good welcome, can make good people.

William Shakespeare, *Henry VIII*

Wine… the intellectual part of the meal.

Alexandre Dumas

I like to drink Martinis. Two, at the most. Three, I'm under the table; four, I'm under the host.

Dorothy Parker

It is well to remember that there are five reasons for drinking: the arrival of a friend; one's present or future thirst; the excellence of the wine; or any other reason.

Latin proverb

Good wine is a necessity of life for me.

Thomas Jefferson

In victory you deserve champagne, in defeat you need it.

Napoleon Bonaparte

Whenever a man is tired,
wine is a great restorer
of strength.

Homer, *The Iliad*

Is the glass half full, or half empty? It depends on whether you're pouring, or drinking.

Bill Cosby

The wine-cup is the little silver well
Where Truth, if Truth there be, doth ever dwell;

Richard Le Gallienne,
Rubáiyát of Omar Khayyám

Sometimes too
much to drink is
barely enough.

Mark Twain

Wine gives a man nothing...
it only puts in motion what
had been locked up in frost.

Samuel Johnson

But I'm not so think as
you drunk I am.

J. C. Squire

Wine is sunlight, held together by water.

Galileo

Red wine is just like ketchup: it goes with everything.

Jason Walton

Alcohol may not solve your
problems, but neither will
water or milk.

Anonymous

Wine rejoices the heart of man and joy is the mother of all virtues.

Johann Wolfgang von Goethe

Alcohol is the anaesthesia
by which we endure the
operation of life.

George Bernard Shaw

On some days, my head is filled with such wild and original thoughts that I can barely utter a word. On other days, the liquor store is closed.

Frank Varano

Drink is the feast of
reason and the flow
of soul.

Alexander Pope

Abstainer: a weak person who yields to the temptation of denying himself a pleasure.

Ambrose Bierce

Wine gives courage
and makes men more
apt for passion.

Ovid

I've never been drunk, but
often I've been over served.

George Gobel

Reality is an illusion
created by a lack
of alcohol.

Anonymous

Even though a number of people have tried, no one has yet found a way to drink for a living.

Jean Kerr

If you drink, don't drive. Don't even putt.

Dean Martin

To happy convents,
bosomed deep in vines,
Where slumber abbots,
purple as their wines.

Alexander Pope, *The Dunciad*

Health – what my friends are always drinking to before they fall down.

Phyllis Diller

Be wary of strong drink. It can make you shoot at tax collectors… and miss.

Robert A. Heinlein

A man's got to believe
in something. I believe
I'll have another drink.

W. C. Fields

The problem with the world is that everyone is a few drinks behind.

Humphrey Bogart

There is a communion of
more than our bodies when
bread is broken and
wine drunk.

M. F. K. Fisher

I never trust a man
that doesn't drink.

John Wayne

I went on a diet, swore off
eating and heavy drinking,
and in fourteen days I lost
two weeks.

Joe E. Lewis

Wine improves with age. The older I get, the better I like it.

Anonymous

Wine makes daily living
easier, less hurried, with
fewer tensions and
more tolerance.

Benjamin Franklin

Wine to me is passion…
Wine is art. It's culture. It's
the essence of civilization
and the art of living.

Robert Mondavi

My only regret is that I did not drink more champagne.

John Maynard Keynes
on his deathbed

Wine is the thinking person's health drink.

Dr Phillip Norrie

I have lived temperately…
I double the doctor's
recommendation of a glass
and a half of wine each day
and even treble it with
a friend.

Thomas Jefferson

Hold the bottle up to the light; you will see your dreams are always at the bottom.

Rob Hutchison

If a life of wine,
women and song
becomes too much,
give up the singing.

Anonymous

Within the bottle's depths, the wine's soul sang one night.

Charles Baudelaire

A gourmet meal without a glass of wine just seems tragic to me somehow.

Kathy Mattea

Happiness is a dry Martini
and a good woman... or a
bad woman.

George Burns

From wine what
sudden friendship
springs.

John Gay, 'Fables'

If God forbade
drinking, would He
have made wine
so good?

Cardinal Richelieu

May our love be like good wine, grow stronger as it grows older.

Old English toast

Eat thy bread with joy,
and drink thy wine
with a merry heart.

Ecclesiastes 9:7

A mind of the calibre of mine
cannot derive its nutrient
from cows.

George Bernard Shaw

Wine gives strength to weary men.

Homer

There is not the hundredth
part of the wine consumed
in this kingdom that there
ought to be. Our foggy
climate wants help.

Jane Austen, *Northanger Abbey*

A woman drove me to drink, and I'll be a son-of-a-gun but I never even wrote to thank her.

W. C. Fields

When a man drinks
wine at dinner, he
begins to be better
pleased with himself.

Plato

One not only drinks
the wine, one smells it,
observes it, tastes it, sips it
and – one talks about it.

King Edward VII

A waltz and a glass of wine invite an encore.

Johann Strauss

My idea of a fine wine
was one that merely
stained my teeth
without stripping
the enamel.

Clive James, *Falling Towards England*

When you ask one
friend to dine,
Give him your best wine!
When you ask two,
The second best will do!

Henry Wadsworth Longfellow

Men are like wine –
some turn to vinegar,
but the best improve
with age.

Pope John XXIII

Wine brings to light the
hidden secrets of the soul,
gives being to our hopes,
bids the coward flight,
drives dull care away, and
teaches new means for the
accomplishment of
our wishes.

Horace

If food is the body of good living, wine is its soul.

Clifton Fadiman

I never taste the wine first in restaurants, I just ask the waiter to pour.

Nigella Lawson

Always carry a
corkscrew and the wine
shall provide itself.

Basil Bunting

In the order named, these are the hardest to control: Wine, Women, and Song.

Franklin P. Adams

Here's to the corkscrew – a useful key to unlock the storehouse of wit, the treasury of laughter, the front door of fellowship and the gate of pleasant folly!

W. E. P. French

If it wasn't for the olives in his Martinis, he'd starve to death.

Milton Berle

Wine is made to be drunk
as women are made to
be loved; profit by the
freshness of youth or the
splendour of maturity; do not
await decrepitude.

Théophile Malvezin

Woman first tempted
man to eat; he took
to drinking of his
own accord.

John R. Kemble

I made wine out of raisins so
I wouldn't have to wait for
it to age.

Steven Wright

Making good wine is a skill; making fine wine is an art.

Robert Mondavi

There are many wines
that taste great, but
do not drink well.

Michael Broadbent

'Twas Noah who first
planted the vine and
mended his morals by
drinking its wine.

Benjamin Franklin

Life is too short to drink bad wine.

Anonymous

Beer is made by men,
wine by God!

Martin Luther

Behold the rain which descends from heaven upon our vineyards, and which incorporates itself with the grapes, to be changed into wine; a constant proof that God loves us, and loves to see us happy.

Benjamin Franklin

Gentlemen, in the little moment that remains to us between the crisis and the catastrophe, we may as well drink a glass of champagne.

Paul Claudel

Wine is the drink of the gods, milk the drink of babes, tea the drink of women, and water the drink of beasts.

John Stuart Blackie

Compromises are
for relationships,
not wine.

Sir Robert Scott Caywood

A man cannot make him laugh – but that's no marvel; he drinks no wine.

William Shakespeare, *King Henry IV*

Wine gives great
pleasure; and every
pleasure is of itself
a good.

Samuel Johnson

What's drinking?
A mere pause
from thinking!

Lord Byron,
The Deformed Transformed

Give me wine to wash me
clean of the weather-stains
of care.

Ralph Waldo Emerson

... fan the sinking flame of hilarity with the wing of friendship; and pass the rosy wine.

Charles Dickens,
The Old Curiosity Shop

Once, during Prohibition, I was forced to live for days on nothing but food and water.

W. C. Fields

The wine urges me on, the bewitching wine, which sets even a wise man to singing and to laughing gently, and rouses him up to dance…

Homer

What Freud was to psychoanalysis, I was to wine.

Sam Aaron

In water one sees one's own face, but in wine one beholds the heart of another.

French proverb

A bottle of good wine,
like a good act, shines
ever in the retrospect.

Robert Louis Stevenson

And wine can of their
wits the wise beguile,
Make the sage frolic,
and the serious smile,

Homer, *The Odyssey*
(translated by Alexander Pope)

Clearly, the pleasures wines afford are transitory – but so are those of the ballet, or of a musical performance. Wine is inspiring and adds greatly to the joy of living.

Napoleon Bonaparte

Where there is no wine there is no love.

Euripides

Wine hath drowned more
men than the sea.

Thomas Fuller

Age is just a number. It's totally irrelevant unless, of course, you happen to be a bottle of wine.

Joan Collins

What is better than to sit
at the table at the end of
the day and drink wine with
friends, or substitutes
for friends?

James Joyce

Wine is a peep-hole
on a man.

Alcaeus

To take wine into our mouths
is to savour a droplet of the
river of human history.

Clifton Fadiman

I like best the wine
drunk at the cost
of others.

Diogenes the Cynic

The smell of wine, oh
how much more delicate,
cheerful, gratifying, celestial
and delicious it is than that
of oil.

François Rabelais

Hide our ignorance as we will, an evening of wine soon reveals it.

Heraclitus

I always knew the importance of it, since I was three or four years old my mother used to feed me wine and water. I grew up with wine as liquid food.

Robert Mondavi

The best use of bad wine is to drive away poor relations.

French proverb

It is the hour to be drunken! To escape being the martyred slaves of time, be ceaselessly drunk. On wine, on poetry, or on virtue, as you wish.

Charles Baudelaire

It is widely held that too much wine will dull a man's desire. Indeed it will in a dull man.

John Osborne

My nose itched, and
I knew I should drink
wine or kiss a fool.

Jonathan Swift

There's something about having a great bottle of wine and a great cigar. Nothing compares to it.

D. L. Hughley

This is the great fault
of wine; it first trips
up the feet: it is a
cunning wrestler.

Plautus

When I put my nose in
a glass, it's like tunnel
vision... every bit of mental
energy is focused on
that wine.

Robert M. Parker, Jr

Happiness is finding two olives in your Martini when you're hungry.

Johnny Carson

God in His goodness sent
the grapes,
To cheer both great
and small;
Little fools will drink
too much,
And great fools not at all.

Anonymous

I am falser than vows
made in wine.

William Shakespeare, *As You Like It*

I drank at every vine.
The last was like the first.
I came upon no wine
So wonderful as thirst.

Edna St Vincent Millay

You don't want to mix emotions up with wine like that. You lose the taste.

Ernest Hemingway

Never did a great man
hate good wine.

François Rabelais

Good wine ruins the purse,
bad wine ruins the stomach.

Spanish proverb

Pour out the wine without
restraint or stay,
Pour not by cups, but by
the bellyful,
Pour out to all that wull.

Edmund Spenser

Wine is life.

Petronius

KEEP
CALM
AND
DRINK
UP

KEEP CALM AND DRINK UP

£4.99

ISBN: 978 1 84953 102 3

'*In victory, you deserve champagne; in defeat, you need it.*'

Napoleon Bonaparte

BAD ADVICE FOR GOOD PEOPLE

Keep Calm and Carry On, a World War Two government poster, struck a chord in recent difficult times when a stiff upper lip and optimistic energy were needed again. But in the long run it's a stiff drink and flowing spirits that keep us all going.

Here's a book packed with proverbs and quotations showing the wisdom to be found at the bottom of the glass.

www.summersdale.com

SAVE
WATER
DRINK
WINE

SAVE
WATER
DRINK
WINE

SAVE
WATER
DRINK
WINE

SAVE
WATER
DRINK
WINE

SAVE
WATER
DRINK
WINE

SAVE
WATER
DRINK
WINE

SAVE
WATER
DRINK
WINE

SAVE
WATER
DRINK
WINE

SAVE SAVE SAVE

ATER WATER WATER WA

INK DRINK DRINK DI

NE WINE WINE WI

SAVE SAVE SAVE

WATER WATER WATER

DRINK DRINK DRINK

WINE WINE WINE

SAVE SAVE SAVE

ATER WATER WATER WA

INK DRINK DRINK DI

NE WINE WINE WI

SAVE SAVE SAVE

WATER WATER WATER

DRINK DRINK DRINK

WINE WINE WINE